LinkedIn Marketing Workbook:

How to Use LinkedIn For Business

2016 Edition

by Jason McDonald, Ph.D.

© 2015-2016, JM Internet Group

https://www.jm-seo.org/

Tel. 800-298-4065

0

INTRODUCTION

Welcome to the *LinkedIn Marketing Workbook, 2016 edition*! Get ready to

- have some **fun**;
- **learn how LinkedIn works;**
- understand how to use **LinkedIn** to **market your business**; and
- create a step-by-step **LinkedIn marketing plan**.

Fully revised and updated for 2016, this workbook not only explains how to market on LinkedIn but also provides access to **free** LinkedIn marketing tools. It provides overviews, step-by-step instructions, tips and secrets, free tools for LinkedIn marketing, and (*wait, there's more!*) access to worksheets that will help you build a systematic LinkedIn marketing plan. Even better, if you register your copy, you also get access to my complete *Social Media Toolbook*, with literally hundreds of free social media marketing tools to turbocharge your social media marketing not just on LinkedIn but also on Facebook, Twitter, YouTube, Google+, Instagram and other major social media platforms.

> *It slices, it dices. It explains how to LinkedIn works. It gives you free tools. And it helps you make a LinkedIn marketing plan.*

If you're really gung-ho for **social media marketing**, I refer you to my *Social Media Workbook*, an all-in-one guide to the entire social media universe from Facebook to LinkedIn, Twitter to YouTube, Instagram to Pinterest, Yelp to Google+, and everything in between. Learn more about that book at http://jmlinks.com/social or call 800-298-4065.

Why Market via LinkedIn?

If you've read this far, you're definitely intrigued by LinkedIn as a marketing platform. Perhaps you're just starting out with a **LinkedIn Profile**, or a **LinkedIn Page** for your **business**. Or perhaps you already have a profile or Page, but want to make them really work. Perhaps you think LinkedIn is only for job-seekers, and you can't see the **business-to-business** marketing opportunities lurking behind the job-seeking noise.

Let's step back for a minute and ask: **why market on LinkedIn**?

Here are some reasons:

- **LinkedIn is big.** LinkedIn is the largest business-to-business, professional social media platform, with over three hundred sixty million users worldwide and climbing.
- **LinkedIn is all about business (to business).** Whereas Facebook is about friends, family and fun, LinkedIn is the "serious" social media. Its users are there for business: to schmooze with each other, to learn about their industry, to search for jobs, and to present themselves (and their companies) in a favorable light.
- **LinkedIn is More than Job Search.** While LinkedIn is justifiably famous for job-seekers, this book is NOT about job search. LinkedIn is full of business-to-business marketing opportunities: ways to find prospects, ways to encourage inbound leads, ways to position yourself and your company as attractive business partners. *If you think LinkedIn is only about job search, you're missing out.*
- **LinkedIn is free**. LinkedIn is, of course, free to use. And in terms of marketing there is a lot you can do, for free, to build your brand, spread eWOM (electronic word of mouth), help you stay top-of-mind with your customers, and even "get shares" or "go viral."
- **LinkedIn has advertising.** If you advertise smart on LinkedIn, and combine paid advertising with free organic LinkedIn marketing, you can demographically target not only your current customers but also prospective customers, thereby radically extending the reach of your online marketing efforts.

LinkedIn, however, is also complicated. Using it is one thing, and marketing on LinkedIn is another. Most businesses fail at LinkedIn marketing because they just don't "get it." They don't understand how LinkedIn works, and they fail to see the incredible marketing opportunities beneath the surface of the job-seekers. Confusingly, LinkedIn works at both person-to-person and a business-to-person levels; many businesses fail to understand this important distinction.

Quite simply, you have to invest some time to learn "how" to market on LinkedIn.

Enter the *LinkedIn Marketing Workbook*.

Who is this Workbook For?

This workbook is aimed primarily at **small business owners** and **marketing managers**. Non-profits will also find it useful. *(Note: this book is NOT for job-seekers, and it does NOT cover LinkedIn for job-seekers, although many job-seekers will find it relevant).*

If you are a person whose job involves advertising, marketing, and/or branding, this workbook is for you. If you are a small business (especially one that sells business-to-business) that sees a marketing opportunity in LinkedIn, this workbook is for you. If your job is customer prospecting (cold calling, cold emailing, and good ole' start the ball rolling prospecting for customers), this workbook is for you. And if your job is to market a business or organization online in today's Internet economy, this book is for you. Anyone who wants to look behind the curtain and understand the mechanics of how to market on LinkedIn will benefit from this book.

Anyone who sees – however dimly – that LinkedIn could help market their business (or themselves as a professional) will benefit from this hands-on guide.

How Does This Workbook Work?

This workbook starts first with an overview to **social media *marketing***. If social media is a **party**, then **using social media** is akin to just *showing up*. **Marketing** on social media, in contrast, isn't about showing up. It's about ***throwing*** the party!

Understanding that distinction between "attending" the social media party and "throwing" the social media party is the subject of **Chapter One.**

Chapter Two is a deep dive into LinkedIn marketing. We'll overview how LinkedIn works, explain everything from profiles to pages, follows to comments to shares, 1st to 2nd level connections and more. It will all become much clearer, as we work through LinkedIn in plain English, written for "mere mortals." Along the way, I'll provide **worksheets** that will act as "Jason as therapist," so you can fill them out and begin to outline your own unique LinkedIn marketing plan, both as an individual and as a company.

Finally, this workbook ends with an **Appendix**: a list of amazing **free LinkedIn tools** and resources. Even better, if you register your copy, you get clickable online access to the tools, a PDF copy of the book, and (wait, there's more!) a complimentary copy of my *Social Media Toolbook*, my compilation of hundreds of social media tools not just for LinkedIn but for all the major platforms.

Here's how to register your copy of this workbook:

1. Go to https://jm-seo.org/workbooks
2. Click on LinkedIn.
3. Use this password: **linkedin2016**
4. You're in. Simply click on the link for a PDF copy of the *Social Media Toolbook* as well as access to the worksheets referenced herein.

OK, now that we know what this workbook is about, who it is for, and our plan of action...

Let's get started!

≫ MEET THE AUTHOR

My name is Jason McDonald, and I have been active on the Internet since 1994 (having invented the Internet along with Al Gore) and taught SEO, AdWords, and Social Media since 2009 – online, at Stanford University Continuing Studies, at both AcademyX and the Bay Area Video Coalition in San Francisco, at workshops, and in corporate trainings across these United States. I love figuring out how things work, and I love teaching others! Social media marketing is an endeavor that I understand, and I want to empower you to understand it as well.

Learn more about me at https://www.jasonmcdonald.org/ or at my corporate website https://www.jm-seo.org/. Or just call 800-298-4065, say something flattering, and I my secretary will put you through. *(Like I have a secretary! Just call if you have something to ask or say)*.

≫ SPREAD THE WORD: WRITE A REVIEW & GET A FREE EBOOK!

If you like this workbook, please take a moment to write an honest review on Amazon.com. *If you hate the book, feel free to trash it on Amazon or anywhere across the Internet. (I have thick skin). If you hate life, in general, and are just one of those bitter people who write bitter reviews... well, gosh, go off and meditate, talk to a priest or do something spiritual. Life is just too short to be that bitter!*

At any rate, here is my special offer for those lively enough to write a review of the book–

1. Write your **honest review** on Amazon.com.
2. **Contact** me via https://www.jm-seo.org/contact and let me know your review is up.
3. Include your **email address** and **website URL**, and any quick questions you have about it.
4. I will send you a **free** copy of one of my other eBooks which cover AdWords, SEO, and Social Media Marketing.

This offer is limited to the first 100 reviewers, and only for reviewers who have purchased a paid copy of the book. You may be required to show proof of purchase and the birth certificate of your first born child, cat, or goldfish. If you don't have a child, cat, or goldfish, you may be required to prove telepathically that you bought the book.

» QUESTIONS AND MORE INFORMATION

I **encourage** my students to ask questions! If you have questions, submit them via https://www.jm-seo.org/contact/. There are two sorts of questions: ones that I know instantly, for which I'll zip you an email answer right away, and ones I do not know instantly, in which case I will investigate and we'll figure out the answer together.

As a teacher, I learn most from my students. So please don't be shy!

» COPYRIGHT AND DISCLAIMER

Uh! Legal stuff! Get ready for some fun:

This is a completely **unofficial** guide to LinkedIn marketing. LinkedIn has not endorsed this guide, nor has anyone affiliated with LinkedIn been involved in the production of this guide.

That's a *good thing*. This guide is **independent**. My aim is to "tell it as I see it," giving you no-nonsense information on how to succeed at LinkedIn marketing.

In addition, please note the following:

- All trademarks are the property of their respective owners. I have no relationship with nor endorsement from the mark holders. Any use of their marks is so I can provide information to you.

- Any reference to or citation of third party products or services whether for LinkedIn, LinkedIn, Twitter, Yelp, Google / Google+, Yahoo, Bing, Pinterest, YouTube, or other businesses, search engines, or social media platforms, should not be construed as an endorsement of those products or services tools, nor as a warranty as to their effectiveness or compliance with the terms of service with any search engine or social media platform.

The information used in this guide was derived in August, 2015. However, social media marketing changes rapidly, so please be aware that scenarios, facts, and conclusions are subject to change without notice.

Additional Disclaimer. Internet marketing is an art, and not a science. Any changes to your Internet marketing strategy, including SEO, Social Media Marketing, and AdWords, is at your own risk. Neither Jason McDonald, Excerpti Communications, Inc., nor the JM Internet Group assumes any responsibility for the effect of any changes you may, or may not, make to your website or AdWords advertising based on the information in this guide.

» ACKNOWLEDGEMENTS

No man is an island. I would like to thank my beloved wife, Noelle Decambra, for helping me hand-in-hand as the world's best moderator for our online classes, and as my personal cheerleader in the book industry. Gloria McNabb has done her usual tireless job as first assistant, including updating this edition as well the *Social Media Marketing* toolbook. Alex Facklis and Hannah McDonald also assisted with tools and research. I would also like to thank my black Labrador retriever, Buddy, for countless walks and games of fetch, during which I refined my ideas about marketing and about life.

And, again, a huge thank you to my students – online, in San Francisco, and at Stanford Continuing Studies. You challenge me, you inspire me, and you motivate me!

LINKEDIN

If **Facebook** is all about friends, family, and fun – a kind of 24/7 fun company picnic to which the general public is invited, **LinkedIn** is akin to your real-world company networking event. If you've ever been to a big trade show such as the *Consumer Electronics Show* in Las Vegas, or the annual *Direct Marketing Association (DMA) show* in Boston, you've likely attended corporate meet-and-greets, wine and cheese sessions, or breakout learning sessions on important industry topics. They feature free food and entertainment, a speech or two by the CEO, and lots of schmoozing between vendors and potential customers. In some cases, actual learning occurs; in others it's all about making professional contacts. Dressed in business casual, people listen attentively, are in "learning" mode, and are also ready to introduce themselves and their products to you and others.

Schmoozing, in short, is the No. 1 activity in LinkedIn marketing.

"Hi, my name is Jason McDonald, what's yours?" It's totally appropriate in this setting to walk up to total strangers and introduce your (business) self; even better is to get one business contact to introduce you to another. *"Hey, Sue, this is Jason McDonald, my social media expert friend. You and he have a lot in common because you're crazy for Twitter, so I'd thought I'd introduce you."* A quick Google search of *define:schmooze* (at http://jmlinks.com/3f), defines it as to *talk, chat up, converse, mingle, hobnob, network, and work the room.* That's the key purpose of LinkedIn in a nutshell: to **schmooze**.

Secondarily, **learning** is an increasingly important purpose on LinkedIn.

LinkedIn recently acquired online learning company, Lynda.com, and LinkedIn *Pulse* is a sort of communal blogging platform on business-to-business trends. Both speak to LinkedIn's focus on continuing education. Attending a trade show is not just about schmoozing, after all; it's also about keeping up with industry trends, and about learning about important industry topics. **Learning**, therefore, is the No. 2 activity of import on LinkedIn.

This chapter will explore **LinkedIn for business**, with one important exception: **job search**. While LinkedIn is THE social platform for job search, we will confine our explanation to the use of LinkedIn by an established company, or employed individual, seeking to reach out to existing and new customers through social media. Our focus is on you as an individual, or you as a company (or you and your employees acting as a team) using LinkedIn to advance your marketing goals: building brand identity, staying in contact with prospects and customers, encouraging social spread, and putting your best foot forward so that you are perceived as a trustworthy business partner.

In this Chapter, will explore the four big marketing opportunities on LinkedIn: 1) setting up your profile (as well as those of your employees) as a public resume, 2) using LinkedIn to research and network with customers and prospects, 3) participating in LinkedIn groups, and 4) leveraging a LinkedIn company page for your business.

Let's get started!

ToDo List:

» Explore how LinkedIn Works

» The LinkedIn Profile as Public Resume

» Schmoozing on LinkedIn: Your Social Rolodex

» Being Active on LinkedIn: Posting and Groups

» LinkedIn Company Pages

» Promoting Your LinkedIn Profile, Posts, and Pages

» Measuring your Results

» Deliverable: a LinkedIn Marketing Plan

» Appendix: Top Ten LinkedIn Marketing Tools and Resources

» EXPLORE HOW LINKEDIN WORKS

Let's review the basic structure of LinkedIn:

- **Individuals have LinkedIn profiles**, which function as online resumes listing skills, education, and interests. Profiles allow one individual to "connect" with another individual; once connected, any post by individual No. 1 will show in the news feed of individual No. 2. In this sense, LinkedIn Profiles function structurally in exactly the same way as Facebook profiles: you send connection requests (friend requests), and once accepted and connected, you and the other individual can directly check each other out, communicate via LinkedIn messaging, and see posts to each other's news feed.
- **Individuals can join groups.** While groups on Facebook are of limited business interest, groups on LinkedIn are very important. As at a major trade show, LinkedIn has "break out" groups by topic (from petroleum engineering to marketing to advertising to WordPress web design and beyond), that bring like-minded people together in a professional way. Note, however, that it is people (and not business Pages!) that participate in groups.
- **Companies can have LinkedIn Pages.** As on Facebook, companies can create business Pages on LinkedIn. Individuals can follow companies, and by doing so, give permission to that company to converse. Posts by the company have a chance to show in the news feed of individuals who have "followed" a particular company.
- **Posts and the News Feed.** When an individual posts to his or her LinkedIn profile, or a company posts to its LinkedIn Page, those posts show up in the news feed of connected individuals. LinkedIn, like Facebook, therefore has a posting rhythm in which individuals and businesses compete for eyeballs and attention.

Structurally, therefore, LinkedIn is very similar to Facebook. *Profiles and connection requests, Pages and following, posts and news feeds.*

However, the **structural** similarities hide a very different **culture** on LinkedIn. Whereas on Facebook, the center of marketing is the business Page. On LinkedIn, the center of gravity lies with the personal profiles of employees. Whereas on Facebook, you primarily interact with business pages in terms of marketing, on LinkedIn you primarily interact with the employees of various businesses.

LINKEDIN'S CENTER OF GRAVITY IS THE PERSONAL PROFILE

LinkedIn's center of gravity is person-to-person interaction. This makes sense if you compare a company picnic (Facebook) with a business networking event (LinkedIn). Whereas at the former, you interact with the company (who brings the food and entertainment, and pays for the party), at the latter, you interact with the employees of the company, talking about industry events and schmoozing about shared interests. You don't business network with *companies*, after all: you business network with *individuals*.

Whereas on Facebook, it's impolite to ask what one "does for a living" or to "pitch business ideas," on LinkedIn this is so important as to be the core function. People on LinkedIn, in short, are in **business networking mode**. This makes it a fantastic social medium for business-to-business marketing!

LinkedIn is the 24/7 business networking event

In addition, LinkedIn groups are rather robust, especially in technical areas. For a technical industry such as oil and gas, people increasingly use LinkedIn groups as a way to stay professionally educated. LinkedIn's acquisition of Lynda.com (http://www.lynda.com/) speaks to this growing trend to use LinkedIn as a way to stay up-to-date about an industry. Finally, although business Pages do exist on LinkedIn and are increasingly important for business-to-business companies, their utility is much weaker than on Facebook for business-to-consumer companies.

LinkedIn is a Team Sport

Perhaps the most important distinction of all is to think of Facebook as a *company-first* marketing platform and LinkedIn as a *team-first* marketing platform. Whereas on Facebook, you can manage your marketing "top down," using your company Page as your primary customer interaction vehicle, on LinkedIn you must rely heavily on your employees. Every customer-facing employee needs to be "on board" with your LinkedIn marketing: he or she needs a robust LinkedIn profile, and a passionate commitment to schmooze with other LinkedIn members through outreach, posting, and group participation. To really succeed at LinkedIn as a business, each and every customer-facing employee must actively participate as an individual, and your company should manage its own LinkedIn business page in tandem. LinkedIn, in sum, is an **employee team sport** (more on this later).

Employee participation + an active ***LinkedIn business page*** = *LinkedIn marketing **success***.

Throughout this Chapter, I will often refer to an individual "you" as participating in LinkedIn, but remember when I say "you," I mean "you" as an individual as well as "you" as a team of like-minded, enthusiastic employees. If your company is one employee, five employees, or five hundred employees, the real key to LinkedIn success is to get everyone "on board" and participating!

Search LinkedIn

First, you'll need to research LinkedIn to estimate its value to your business marketing efforts. (We'll assume you've already set up a basic personal profile on LinkedIn. If not, visit https://www.linkedin.com/ and sign up). For your first Todo, log on to LinkedIn, and search by keywords that are relevant to your company or industry. Identify persons, groups, and companies that are active on these topics.

Simply type a keyword of interest into the search bar at the top of the LinkedIn page (e.g., "organic food" if your company is involved in the organic industry, or "oil and gas," if your company works in the petroleum industry). On the left, click on people, jobs, companies, groups, universities, or posts, to narrow down your search and browse what's going on.

Here's a screenshot:

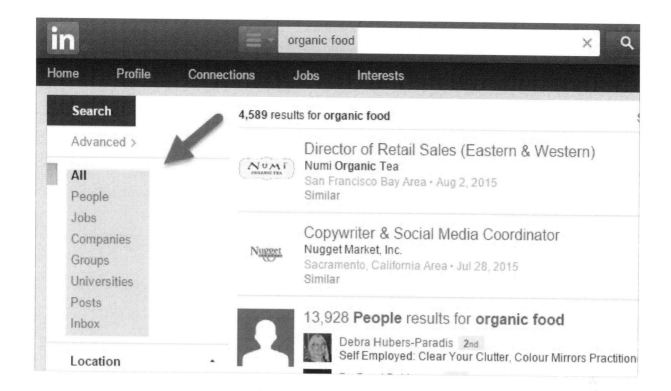

As you begin touring LinkedIn with the question of whether (or not) your potential customers actively use it, narrow your search by type, and ask these questions:

People. Do you see many people with relevant job skills and active profiles on LinkedIn? You're not looking to hire them; you're looking to see if your target customers are engaged enough on LinkedIn to be actively updating their profiles and posting to their accounts. Are they active on LinkedIn?

Companies. Especially for business-to-business sectors, LinkedIn company pages can be quite robust. Are your competitors on LinkedIn? Are similar companies? If so, what are they doing? If not, why not? Do you see a lot (or a little) interaction on the company pages?

Groups. LinkedIn groups act like breakout sessions at a trade show. Do you see relevant groups on LinkedIn? Are they active with many members, or dormant with few? What kinds of discussions are going on?

Posts. Who is posting on relevant topics on LinkedIn and why? What is the quality of the posts, and are there many comments, and reshares to specific posts?

As is always the case in social media, there's no point in pouring time, treasure, and talent into LinkedIn marketing if you don't see your customers online. But if you do, then it will be well worth the effort.

For your first TODO, download the **LinkedIn Research Worksheet**. For the worksheet, go to https://www.jm-seo.org/workbooks (click on LinkedIn, enter the code 'linkedin2016' to register if you have not already done so), and click on the link to the "LinkedIn Research Worksheet." You'll answer questions as to whether your potential customers are on LinkedIn, identify individuals and companies to follow, and inventory what you like and dislike about their LinkedIn set up and marketing strategy.

» THE LINKEDIN PROFILE AS PUBLIC RESUME

The personal profile is the foundation of LinkedIn. Just as on Facebook, an individual needs to set up a LinkedIn profile and populate it with information about him or herself. Unlike on Facebook, however, this personal profile is highly visible and acts as a kind of "public resume." As a business owner or marketer, you'll want your own well-optimized profile, but you'll also want to motivate your CEO, other key executives, and any employees that are customer-facing to potential clients to also set up and optimize their LinkedIn profiles.

The TODOS here are:

1. **Sign up** for LinkedIn as a personal profile.
2. Identify the **keywords** that represent your business value to other people, that is keywords that "describe you" as a businessperson and/or a company or non-profit, such as "WordPress web designer," "CPA," or "Business Coach for startups," or "Apple iPhone App development firm."
3. **Optimize** your personal profile so that it –
   a. Clearly and quickly represents your **personal business value proposition** as well as that of your **company**.
   b. Is **findable** via LinkedIn search by **keywords**.
   c. Establishes **trust** in you as an authority and someone who is worthy of a business partnership.

First and foremost, think of **search** and **trust**. By search, we mean that people will go to Google and/or LinkedIn after they have met you. They'll "search" you on the Internet with an eye to deciding whether you have any skeletons in your closet, whether you seem knowledgeable about your subject, and whether you seem like a good person to do business with. Nowadays, people go to networking events such as trade shows, and return with business cards and email addresses. They then "vet" these people by searching them on Google and on LinkedIn. Indeed, you can optimize your LinkedIn profile to show high on searches for your own name plus keywords.

Think of your LinkedIn profile as your public resume.

To see mine, visit http://jmlinks.com/3g. Note that my LinkedIn profile appears in about position four on a Google search for *Jason McDonald SEO*. Here's a screenshot:

Jason McDonald | LinkedIn
https://www.linkedin.com/in/jasoneg3 ▾
San Francisco Bay Area - SEO, AdWords & Social Media Consulting & Expert Witness
- San Francisco Bay Area
View Jason McDonald's professional profile on LinkedIn. LinkedIn is the ... SEO,
AdWords & Social Media Consulting & Expert Witness - San Francisco Bay Area.

The concept here is when someone meets me (or meets you, or meets a key employee), you want to use LinkedIn to show prominently in a search for your name plus keywords, plus you want your LinkedIn profile to show off your expertise and talents. Just like a "real" resume, your LinkedIn "resume" should be optimized to be found and to put your best foot forward. It should also be publically viewable without the necessity of being logged into LinkedIn.

In short, optimize the LinkedIn profiles of **all** key, customer-facing employees. LinkedIn is a team sport: you need every employee "on board" with full participation.

Now, let's turn to the steps to **optimize** a LinkedIn profile for search and trust.

Define your target keywords. What value do you provide for others in a business relationship? Remember: you are NOT looking for a job. Generally, you are positioning yourself as a "helpful expert" in a defined area. Are you a WordPress expert? An expert CPA for small business? An architect with a focus on ecofriendly design? Brainstorm and define the logical keywords that someone would append to your name. There are, for example, many "Jason McDonalds" in this world. But I want to rank, and be trusted as the Jason McDonald that can help you with **SEO**, **Social Media**, and **AdWords**. Thus, I embed those keywords in my profile, and write it well enough to convey my value as a helpful expert in those endeavors.

Once you have identified your keywords, weave them strategically into your LinkedIn profile.

To access these features, click on *profile > edit profile* while logged in to LinkedIn. Hover over an area, and click on the pencil to edit.

Professional Headline. This is the most important text on your LinkedIn profile for search discoverability. It should answer the question, "What can you do for me." Here's a screenshot of mine:

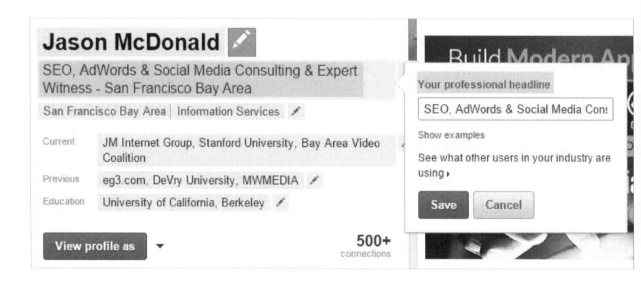

Current (Position). This is your current job, so state it well.

Summary. Like a real resume, this describes your skills and experience. *Do NOT write this like you are looking for a job, if you are NOT looking for a job!* Instead, use ALL CAPS and other ways to break up the content.

Populate it with relevant keywords that people might search on LinkedIn, and make it easy to read. It should state your business value proposition succinctly. Write this "as if" you were explaining to someone at a business networking event what you do, and how this is relevant for what they might need.

Experience. Here's where you input your current and past employment. If your employer is on LinkedIn with a company page, a logo will be available. Again, write succinct summaries of current and past employment that contain logical keywords (do not overdo this), and explain how you can help an interested party to accomplish something of business value.

Languages. Input any languages you speak.

Education. Don't be shy. Populate your education section with your educational achievements, not only degrees but any awards or extra-curricular activities.

Additional Info. Fill out as indicated, especially the "advice for contacting" so that it's easy for prospects to find you.

Honors and Awards. Got any? Add them.

Groups. LinkedIn groups to which you are a member will show here.

A word about groups. At this point, we are optimizing your LinkedIn profile for **search** and **trust**. In terms of groups, therefore, you might consider joining groups not because you plan to actively participate in them but because they convey your interests and skills. For example, I am a member of both the Harvard and UC Berkeley alumni associations really just to convey that I am smart, and attended these prestigious institutions. Similarly, I am a member of Ad Age and WordPress experts groups to convey my interest and expertise in those topics. (I don't actually participate in these groups in any serious way – I'm too busy!) Think of groups as you would think of college extracurricular activities on your resume: to convey interests and skill.

Profile Visibility

At this point, scroll back up, just under the blue "View profile as" button and click on gear icon, next to the the little LinkedIn logo on the left with the https:// web link. Here's a screenshot:

By clicking on the gear icon, you open up the privacy settings of LinkedIn. These appear on the right hand side.

> **Your public profile URL.** Set this to be something short and easy to remember; this becomes what is visible on a Google search.

> **Customize your Public Profile**. Here, you can control what is viewable to anyone either on LinkedIn or via a Google search.

> **Your public profile badge**. Click here, and LinkedIn will give you the code to place on your blog or website, so people can easily view your profile. To see it in action, visit https://www.jasonmcdonald.org/ and click on the LinkedIn icon on the right.

A word about privacy. For most of us, we want to be highly **visible** *(non-private)* on LinkedIn. We want potential customers, friends, and business associates to easily find us. Therefore, set your public profile as "visible to everyone," and check all of the boxes below. *If, for some reason, you do NOT want to be publically visible on LinkedIn, then set the visibility and check boxes accordingly.*

One of the more common mistakes people make is to think of the LinkedIn profile like the Facebook profile: whereas on Facebook, you often want to be *invisible / private* to strangers, on LinkedIn you often want to be *visible / public* to strangers. Accordingly, setting your LinkedIn to private defeats the purposes of search and trust as part of your LinkedIn marketing. For most people, therefore, I recommend to set LinkedIn to fully *visible / public*.

Generally, LinkedIn is *PUBLIC* Profile & *PUBLIC* Company, while Facebook is *PRIVATE* Profile & *PUBLIC* Company

Now close your settings window, go back to the basic profile page, and click on "Contact info" on the far right. Here, you'll see your email, phone, IM, and address as well as social media links. Here's a screenshot:

Generally, I would not put your physical address here (*too many crazy stalkers on the Internet*), but I would put your email and phone. As for the social icons, LinkedIn has a direct link to your Twitter account. As for websites, you can either use their standard descriptions, or if you click "other" you can set these to what you like. I have set mine, for example, to "Contact Jason," "Read Jason's Blog," and "Follow Jason on G+." Here's a screenshot:

You'll need to know the http:// link for each. When enabled, this makes it easy for anyone to contact you on LinkedIn. Importantly, this means that anyone will be able to contact you: 1st level, 2nd level, and even 3rd level connections. If you leave these items blank, then only 1st-level connections will be able to easily contact you via LinkedIn.

Therefore:

> *If you want to be highly findable and easy-to-reach via LinkedIn, be sure to enable the Websites section under your contact information.*

At that point, you're done with populating and optimizing your LinkedIn profile for **search** and **trust**. Congratulate yourself: you've optimized your LinkedIn public resume!

For your second **TODO**, download the **LinkedIn Profile Worksheet**. For the worksheet, go to https://www.jm-seo.org/workbooks (click on LinkedIn, enter the code 'linkedin2016' to register if you have not already done so), and click on the link to the "LinkedIn Profile Worksheet." You'll answer questions to help you set up and optimize your LinkedIn Profile.

Note: as we will discuss below, if you have several "outward-facing" employees, it's an excellent idea to sit down as a company group and have a LinkedIn optimization worksheet. Have each and every important employee optimize his or her LinkedIn profile.

Recommendations and Endorsements

While building out your profile, you'll notice that some people have many **recommendations** or **endorsements**. **Recommendations**, like references for a resume, are generally all positive. After all, you control them: why ask for a reference from a boss or coworker who won't give you a glowing endorsement? Similarly, LinkedIn will prompt you (and your connections) to complete **endorsements** for each other concerning relevant skills. These build out like "merit badges" on your profile, making you look trustworthy.

Note: you control whether recommendations show on your public profile; you can suppress any you do not like.

Solicit Recommendations and Endorsements

Your TODO here is to ask for recommendations and endorsements from friends, coworkers, and business colleagues. One of the best ways to get them is to pro-actively do them for other people. After completing a project with an outside vendor, for example, connect to that person on LinkedIn and write him or her a glowing recommendation and endorsement. Often, they will reciprocate. *(This is called "pre-emptive" recommendations in LinkedIn lingo.)* Regardless of how you get them, getting many positive recommendations and endorsements will make your LinkedIn profile shine.

≫ SCHMOOZING ON LINKEDIN: YOUR SOCIAL ROLADEX

Nearly everyone needs an optimized personal profile on LinkedIn, if for no other purpose than job search. For those whose job is "client or customer facing," meaning identifying, interacting, and schmoozing with potential clients, the primary purpose of LinkedIn is to schmooze. (Schmoozing, of course, is another word for business networking: expanding your circle of business contacts, nurturing their respect for you, and keeping top of mind so that when they have a business opportunity, they think of you).

By nurturing your 1st level contacts and being active on LinkedIn, you can use LinkedIn as your online social rolodex, extending beyond just people you actually know to people you'd like to know for your business needs. Let's investigate schmoozing on LinkedIn, namely:

> **1st level contacts**: these are people who have accepted your connection requests on LinkedIn.

2nd level contacts: these are 1st level contacts of your 1st level contacts (friends of friends, as it were).

LinkedIn Connections: What's Your Bacon Number?

Your "bacon number" is a term coined to humorously point out that nearly everyone on the planet is connected to actor Kevin Bacon. Google, for example, has a funny hidden Easter egg: go to Google and type in a famous person's name followed by "bacon number," for example: "Cher Bacon Number" or visit http://jmlinks.com/3h. Cher has a Bacon number of two because she and Jack Nicholson appeared in *The Witches of Eastwick*, and Jack Nicholson and Kevin Bacon appeared in *A Few Good Men*.

So Cher is a 1st level connection with Jack Nicholson, and a 2nd level connection with Kevin Bacon.

How does the Bacon number concept relate to LinkedIn? LinkedIn uses the same system universally: you can *direct message* or *see the email* of your 1st level connections, and you can use your 1st level connections to get introduced to your 2nd level, for example:

Cher can message via LinkedIn or email Jack Nicholson, directly.

Cher can "see" that Jack Nicholson is connected to Kevin Bacon, and ask Jack to "introduce" her to Kevin.

Similarly, on LinkedIn, you can directly message / find the email of anyone who is your 1st level connection. Or, you can ask a 1st level connection to introduce you to a 2nd level connection. For example, simply search on LinkedIn for the name of someone with whom you are already connected. Then:

Click on the **blue** "Send a message" box. This sends them a message via LinkedIn, and in most cases, will also send them an email alert that they have a message waiting on LinkedIn.

or –

Click on the "**Contact info**" tab and you can view their email address, phone number, and address.

Or, let's assume you're trying to find a connection that has a particular interest or skill. Rather than typing a person's name into the search box, type a keyword / keyphrase such as "WordPress," or "Joomla," or "Accountant for small business" and hit search. On the left, under search you can narrow your results by parameters. Here's a screenshot:

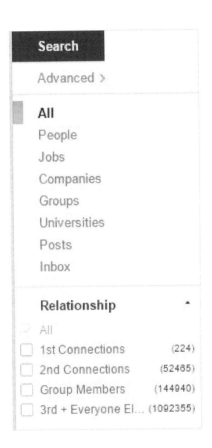

If, for example, click on "People," you are only searching LinkedIn for people whose profiles contain that keyword. If you click on "People," and on "1st Connections," then you are searching for people whose profiles contain the keyword AND are in a 1st level connection with you. Remember: 1st level connections mean you can direct message them via LinkedIn and/or see their email address and other contact information.

You can "tag" 1st level connections by affixing keywords to individual connections. For example, you can create a "tag" that indicates a "real-world friend" or a "tag" that indicates an industry trade show connection or a "tag" that indicates they have a blog. Once tagged, you can then sort or filter your connections by tag. To "tag" a connection, simply click on a connection, click on the "relationship" tab, and next click on "Tag." Here's a screenshot:

Once you've "tagged" your connections, you can then filter them. To do so, click on Connections, and then "Filter by." Here's a screenshot:

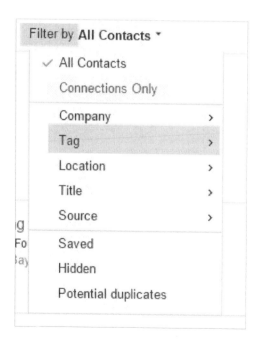

Next, if you like you can message these contacts "as a group." Simply click "select all" and then "Message." This is akin to sending a mass email. When you're doing this, you can send one message to all contacts in a "tag group." If you like you can hide their email addresses / names from each other by unchecking the box "Allow recipients to see each other's names and email addresses." Here's a screenshot:

Essentially, you are able to use LinkedIn as a searchable rolodex of 1ˢᵗ and 2ⁿᵈ level business contacts: define what type of person you want to contact (or prospect), search for them, and reach out directly.

Working with 2ⁿᵈ Level Connections

While you can direct message (send emails or see the email addresses of) 1ˢᵗ level connections, this is not true of 2ⁿᵈ level connections (who are the 1ˢᵗ level connections of your 1ˢᵗ level connections). However, LinkedIn allows you to ask for an "introduction" from a 1ˢᵗ level connection to a 2ⁿᵈ level connection.

Here's a typical scenario.

Let's suppose you are the sale manager for a company in the Proteomics industry. (Proteomics is the large scale study of proteins and is used heavily in industry to analyze organic materials). You're going to "Proteomics World" in Boston, and you'll be introducing your new "Proteomics 2000" product to the industry. You are planning on having one of those fun-filled wine and cheese parties, where your company will roll out the red carpet with free food and wine, and in exchange, attendees will be updated on your "Proteomics 2000." It's a business meeting with a little fun, a little free food and drink, and some salesy information about your new product.

Your job is to get people to attend. You go to LinkedIn and search for:

Proteomics
Check: People
Check: 1ˢᵗ level

You can direct message all of these 1ˢᵗ level people and invite them to the wine and cheese event. Remember: social media is a party, not a prison, and in terms of content you have something fun and interesting: your wine and cheese event.

Secondarily, you can search for

Proteomics
Check: People
Check: 2ⁿᵈ level

Here, although you cannot see the contact information on the 2ⁿᵈ level connections, you can ask for an introduction from a 1ˢᵗ level connection. This is akin to being at a trade show event, going up to a 1ˢᵗ level connection who knows someone whom you want to get to know, and asking for an introduction. Then your 1ˢᵗ level walks over to your 2ⁿᵈ level (his 1ˢᵗ level), and introduces you. Susan (your 1ˢᵗ level) introduces you to Bob (her 1ˢᵗ level, and your 2ⁿᵈ level connection):

> *"Hey Bob, I'd like you to meet Jason. He's the Proteomics marketing manager over at PT Inc. They're having some sort of a wine and cheese event, and I thought you two might get to know each other."*

Or structurally:

> *First level > reason to ask for an introduction > introduction to 2ⁿᵈ level > and (hopefully) the 2ⁿᵈ level becomes a 1ˢᵗ level (accepts your request).*

Essentially, do your search, use the chevron (pull down menu) next to the blue **connect**, and select "Get introduced." Here's a screenshot:

After you click on "Get Introduced," you'll be able to select which 1st level connection you're going to ask for the introduction to the 2nd level connection, and what message you are going to send to them. Here's a screenshot:

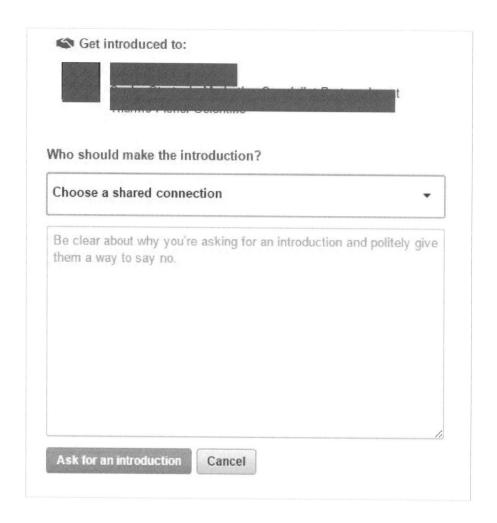

Alternatively, you can send an InMail (see http://jmlinks.com/3m) with a paid account, but it's probably more effective to "get introduced" as it would be in a real-world business encounter. After all, people trust people they know more than a "cold" call or a "cold" InMail / email.

> *It's not what you know (in business). It's who you know.*

The bottom line, therefore, is to use your 1st level connections to get to your 2nd levels, and the **TODO** for LinkedIn is to constantly be expanding your 1st level network, but how?

How to Expand Your LinkedIn Connections

If having many connections is the name of the game on LinkedIn, how do you grow your connections? Here are some strategies:

Ask. Continually ask every business person you meet for their email, and then look them up on LinkedIn. Next click the Connect button and then fill out the information as indicated (you'll need their email and then write a note as to how you met them). Here's a screenshot:

✉ Invite **Sallie** to connect on LinkedIn

Sallie's email address:

`[                              ]` (?)

Include a personal note: (optional)

I'd like to add you to my professional network on LinkedIn.

-Jason

Important: Only invite people you know well and who know you. Find out why.

`Send Invitation` or Cancel

I recommend customizing your personal notes, such as "*Hi Sallie! You and I met at Proteomics world last week, and I'd like to contact with you on LinkedIn.*" If she accepts, she becomes a 1st level connection.

No Spamming. Do not contact people you do not know because spamming LinkedIn can lead your account to be deactivated.

Lifetime Limit. Indeed, there is a lifetime limit of 5000 invitation requests, designed to prevent connection spamming.

Get People to Ask You. Even better than asking people to connect to you, is to get them to ask you. Ideas for this would be:

- **Real World to LinkedIn**. If you give a presentation at a trade show, ask attendees to connect with you on LinkedIn. Include LinkedIn on your business cards, and literally mention LinkedIn when you meet business associates in real life.
- **Your Website or Blog**. Place the LinkedIn icon on your website or blog, and encourage visitors to connect.
- **Other Social Media**. Connect your LinkedIn to your Twitter, Facebook, Google+, etc., and encourage people who already follow you on Twitter, for example, to connect with you on LinkedIn.

The point is to do everything you can to encourage business contacts to connect with you on LinkedIn, because the more you grow your 1st level contacts, the more you can directly connect to them, and the more you can use them as introductions to their 1st level contacts, i.e., your 2nd level contacts.

With Whom Should You Connect?

There are different strategies in terms of reaching out, or accepting, the connection requests of others on LinkedIn. There is no right answer. For someone who is in customer outreach (e.g. sales), he or she should probably accept every inbound request. For someone who is a venture capitalist, he or she might accept requests only from people they really know. Another strategy is to only accept requests from people for whom you'd actually do a favor in real life.

Are Paid LinkedIn Accounts Worth It?

Unless you are an active recruiter, an active job seeker, or an outbound sales person actively "cold calling" or prospecting, I do not generally recommend paid LinkedIn accounts. The main advantages of a paid LinkedIn account (of which there are several types) are:

- Enhanced cosmetics for your profile, such as a larger photo;
- Better positioning when applying for a job;
- Access to everyone who's viewed your profile in the last 90 days;
- Ability to see 3rd degree profiles;

- Additional search filters, and the ability to filter and save search results (great for sales prospectors);
- Up to 10 - 15 InMails per month to directly contact anyone on LinkedIn, even if you are not connected; and/or (depending on the package you get)
- More detailed analytics.

To learn more about LinkedIn Premium, visit https://premium.linkedin.com/. For a very helpful comparison of accounts, visit http://jmlinks.com/3n.

Your **TODO** here is to brainstorm a logical connection philosophy. If your purpose on LinkedIn is to use it for customer outreach and heavy schmoozing, then connecting with anyone or everyone makes sense. If your purpose is more passive or more secretive, perhaps just using LinkedIn as a public resume, and/or to keep up-to-date on industry trends, then connecting only with real-world connections makes sense. Remember: once you accept a connection request, you become a 1st level connection, meaning that person can directly contact you via LinkedIn and email, as well as see your contact information. Similarly, he or she can see your 2nd level connections (unless you block that in settings). So, if you need to be more secretive, then be more judicious about with whom you connect. If not, not. There is no right or wrong connection strategy: just pre-think a strategy that makes sense for your marketing objectives.

Brainstorming a Schmoozing Strategy

For your third **TODO**, download the **LinkedIn Schmoozing Worksheet**. For the worksheet, go to https://www.jm-seo.org/workbooks (click on LinkedIn, enter the code 'linkedin2016' to register if you have not already done so), and click on the link to the "LinkedIn Schmoozing Worksheet." You'll brainstorm your strategy for growing your LinkedIn connections.

» BEING ACTIVE ON LINKEDIN: UPDATES & POSTS

In the real world of business, it's a truism of marketing that you need to "look active." People respect people who are involved and engaged, and look down on people who seem to be doing nothing. Similarly, on LinkedIn it is important to present at least the appearance of activity. By being active, you "look active" (a **trust** indicator) plus you have new ways to reach out to prospects and customers to stay top-of-mind and generate business inquiries.

Posting frequently and being active in LinkedIn groups, in short: a) makes you seem active (and therefore trustworthy), and b) gives you more opportunities to be top of mind among prospects, thereby increasing opportunities for connections and business engagements. I'm not saying you should be fraudulent. But, just as at a business networking event, be active and engaged in a serious way. Participation is important!

Remember: LinkedIn is a team sport, and only individuals can post to their own accounts. Getting employees to post and be active is yet another example why getting all your customer-facing employees "on board" is a key element of LinkedIn success!

Updates and Posts

The first way to do this is to post informative content to LinkedIn on a regular basis via *updates* and *posts*, and the second, is to participate in LinkedIn Groups. Let's look at each in turn.

Just as on Facebook, if you share an update to your profile (what most of us would call a "post," although in LinkedIn lingo this is called an "update,") and I am a 1st level connection, then that post has a good chance of showing in my news feed. The news feed on LinkedIn is the first content that greets me when I login.

Here's a screenshot of my news feed highlighted in yellow:

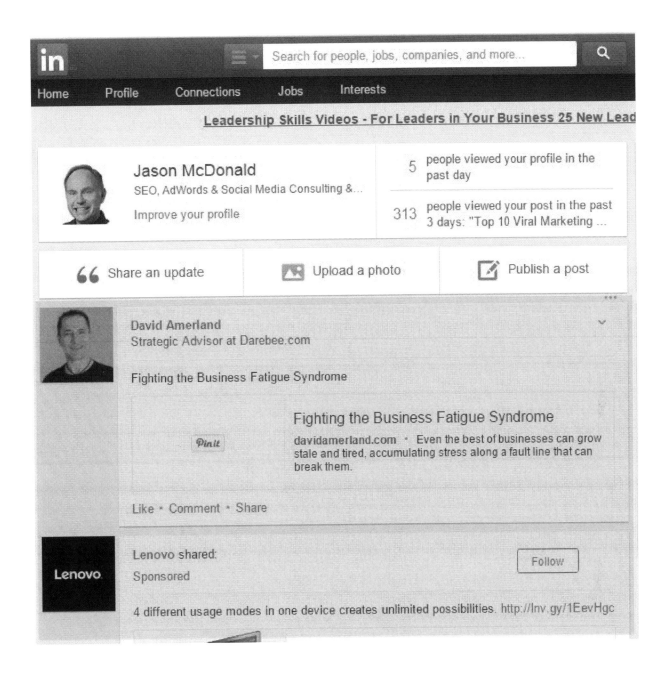

David Amerland, with whom I am a 1st level contact, posted an update, namely a link on LinkedIn to his blog post on "Business Fatigue." He posted his update, and it showed in my news feed. So the process is:

Identify items of interest to your business contacts (your own content or that of others) > Post updates on them to LinkedIn > Your connections see them in their news feeds (and hopefully get excited about doing business with you and/or your company).

Content is king, and queen, and jack on LinkedIn as on all social media. Turn back to your Content Marketing plan, and remember you'll need both other people's content and your own content to post as updates or as posts to *Pulse* (more below):

- **Blog Post Summaries**. To the extent that you have an active blog and are posting items that fit with LinkedIn's professional focus, post headlines, short summaries and links to your blog.
  - Note that the first or "featured" image will become the shareable image, and that the META DESCRIPTION will become the default description when sharing. Choose striking, fun images for your blog posts!
- **Quotes**. People love quotes, and taking memorable quotes (on business themes) and pasting them on graphics is a win/win.
- **Infographics and Instructographics**. Factoids, how to articles, top ten lists, 7 things you didn't know lists, especially ones that are fun yet useful, are excellent for LinkedIn.
- **Quizzes, Surveys, and Response-provoking posts**. Ask a question, and get an answer or more. Great for encouraging interactivity, especially when the interaction is business-oriented. A great idea is to mention a project you are working on, and ask for feedback before, during, or after.

Turn to the content marketing section of the *Social Media Toolbook* for a list of tools that will help you find other people's content and create your own. I recommend Hootsuite (https://www.hootsuite.com/) to manage all your social postings across platforms. I recommend Feedly (http://www.feedly.com/) as a way to organize industry blogs and the content of other people, so that you can be a useful sharer of third-party information on LinkedIn.

LinkedIn *Pulse*

One opportunity not to be missed on LinkedIn in terms of posting is *LinkedIn Pulse* (https://www.linkedin.com/pulse). LinkedIn is aggressively trying to grow its role not only for job seekers but for the fully employed. *Pulse* is LinkedIn's internal blog, and anyone (including you) can easily post to *Pulse*. Think of posting to *Pulse* as you would posting to your own blog:

1. **Identify a topic** that will interest your prospects and customers, such as an industry trend or a common "pain point" in your industry or more generally in business.
2. **Brainstorm and identify keywords** using tools like Google suggest, Ubersuggest, or the Google Keyword Planner.
3. **Write a strong post with a great headline**, catchy first paragraph, and some substantial content that will be useful to readers and position you as a "helpful expert."
4. **Tag your *Pulse* post with relevant tags** – these influence whether your *Pulse* post will show in their news feed and/or relevant searches.

Inside of LinkedIn, *Pulse* lives under the beige button "*+Write a new post*". Here's a screenshot:

Pulse Reaches Beyond Your Connections

LinkedIn *Pulse* also allows individuals with whom you are NOT 1st level connections on LinkedIn to "follow you." Even better, when you share your *Pulse* Post on other social networks (e.g., Twitter, Facebook, Google+) and encourage people to cross over to

LinkedIn, LinkedIn monitors this activity. If you get enough momentum, a *Pulse* Post can "go viral," and really supercharge your LinkedIn connections.

Therefore, a strong *Pulse* posting strategy can position you as a "helpful expert" to new people, and is not an opportunity to be missed!

For your fourth **TODO**, download the **LinkedIn Posting Worksheet**. For the worksheet, go to https://www.jm-seo.org/workbooks (click on LinkedIn, enter the code 'linkedin2016' to register if you have not already done so), and click on the link to the "LinkedIn Posting Worksheet." You'll create a systematic plan for posts to LinkedIn, both your own content and the content of others.

As much as it is fun and easy to post, the reality of LinkedIn today is that outside of job seekers, not everybody checks LinkedIn on a daily or even weekly basis. So while posting frequently to LinkedIn is a good idea, it is not nearly as dynamic as Facebook in terms of active engagement. Keep that in mind when you measure the ROI of posting frequently on LinkedIn.

How frequently should you post?

Now that the LinkedIn news feed is very crowded (and the reality is that only few people outside of job seekers and outbound marketers check their feed daily), you can safely post quite frequently: even several times a day. But this differs with your audience, so pay attention to your updates, by monitoring thumbs up and comments (*for LinkedIn updates*) and stats (*for Pulse posts*). Your goal is to be interesting, informative, useful, and friendly as trust indicators and hopefully get social spread amongst new contacts, especially via *Pulse*. Note that you can see who responded to your *Pulse* posts, and this gives you an opportunity to connect with them

» BEING ACTIVE ON LINKEDIN: LINKEDIN GROUPS

With LinkedIn's growing emphasis on "professional learning," it should come as no surprise that LinkedIn has a growing ecosystem of groups on every topic imaginable. Compare LinkedIn groups to the "break out" sessions at your industry trade show: interested parties show up, listen to each other, participate in discussions, and showcase their questions (and answers) on professional topics. Oh, and occasionally, they use groups as yet another opportunity to **schmooze** *(surprise!)*. By participating tactfully in LinkedIn groups you can grow your prestige (and that of your company). It's a soft sell environment; however, anyone who is a member of a group that you are a member of is a good prospect to become a LinkedIn 1st level connection.

To find relevant groups, simply search LinkedIn by keyword and then click on "Groups" on the left hand column. LinkedIn will return a list of relevant groups; simply click on the group to learn more about it, or click the blue join group.

Note that there are two types of groups: **closed** and **open**. **Closed** groups are indicated by a padlock; by clicking "join," you are requesting the group moderator to approve your membership. **Open** groups lack the padlock icon, and you first click the blue "View" button and then join the group (instantly, no approval required). Once you've joined a group, you'll see a blue "**Post** icon."

Here's a screenshot of the three possibilities, after a keyword search for "content marketing" > groups:

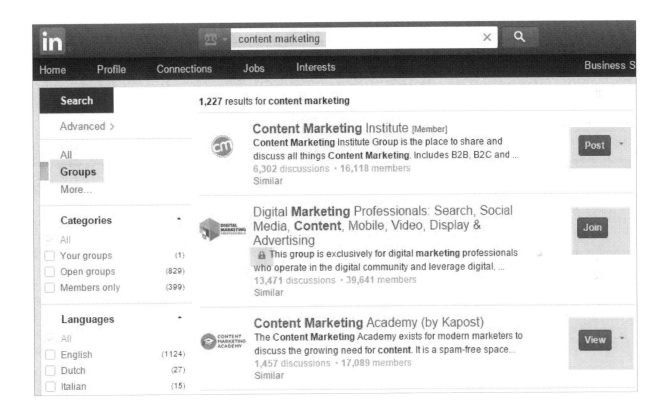

Group Promotion Strategy

LinkedIn is a serious social media platform; so please don't "spam" groups with self-serving "buy my stuff" messages! Instead, join relevant groups, pay attention to the on-going discussions, and post informative and useful content. It's a soft sell environment: let group members realize how smart and useful you are, and then reach out to you directly.

As you research (or join) groups, pay attention to the quality of the discussions. Some groups are fantastic: full of motivated, informed, honest people. Other groups are quite spammy with everyone talking, and few people listening. Just as at a professional trade show, be choosy with your time and efforts. Not all groups are created equally.

Your **TODO** for groups is simple:

- **Log on** to your LinkedIn account.
- **Search for relevant groups** by keyword.
- **Identify** interesting and useful **groups**, and join them (or apply to join if it's a closed group).
- **Monitor** and begin to **participate**.
- Diplomatically position yourself (and your company) as a **helpful expert**.

» LINKEDIN COMPANY PAGES

Like Facebook, LinkedIn offers company Pages. And like Facebook, you must first have an individual profile to create (or manage) a company page. To view the official LinkedIn information on company pages, visit http://jmlinks.com/3h. The steps to create a business Page on LinkedIn are:

1. Sign in to your personal profile.
2. Click on http://jmlinks.com/3j.
3. Add your company name, and your email address, matching the company website domain.
4. Enter your company name.
5. Enter your designated Admins.

Now that you have created a company Page, it's time to optimize it. Login in, first, to your personal profile. Then simply type your company name into the search box. Assuming you are an Admin for your company, LinkedIn will load your company page. On the far right, click on the blue "Edit" button.

Here's a screenshot:

Now you can edit / optimize:

- **Company Name**. Enter or adjust your company name, accordingly.
- **Company Description**. Enter a keyword-heavy yet relevant description of your company. Explain your value proposition: what can you do for LinkedIn members?
- **Designated Admins**. Here, you can add or remove Admins. Any Admin has full control of the page; so if you terminate an employee, remove them first!
- **Image**. Similar to the Facebook cover photo, you can change your LinkedIn (cover) image.
- **Company Logo**. Similar to the Facebook profile picture, you can change your LinkedIn Profile picture.
- **Company Specialties**. These function as keywords for indexing purposes.
- **Featured Groups**. You can feature relevant groups, just as you would at the individual level.

The reality is that few people "search" LinkedIn to find companies. So the bread-and-butter of your company page is to post interesting items (both your own content and that of other people) to people who follow your page because externally they have already decided to follow you. For example, existing customers or people who find your blog interesting might "follow" your company on LinkedIn to stay updated.

For tips from LinkedIn on how to nurture effective company Pages, please visit http://jmlinks.com/3k.

Page Posting Strategy

Although most of the action on LinkedIn is at the profile to profile level, you can post via your company Page as well. Just as with a profile, the trick is to identify interesting, engaging content (both your own and that of others) to post to the Page. In reality, you can cross-post content on both employee profiles and the company page. For example, if the director of marketing writes an informative piece for LinkedIn *Pulse*, you can "cross post" this to your LinkedIn company feed. Similarly, you can identify interesting industry-related articles on Feedly, and share this content at both the profile and Page level.

Essentially, you are trying to position your company as a "helpful expert" on a relevant topic, by posting:

- **Your own content** such as blog posts, videos on YouTube, infographics / instructographics, reports, eBooks, industry studies that deal with industry issues in an informative way;
- **Other people's content** similar to the above.
- **Self-promotional content** like announcements of free Webinars, eBooks, upcoming trade shows, new products, etc.

Remember, of course, your **posting rhythm** of *fun, fun, fun, fun, buy my stuff* (on Facebook), which becomes on LinkedIn:

> *useful, useful, useful, useful, useful, useful, useful, attend our webinar, useful, useful, useful, useful, useful, useful, useful, download our free eBook, useful, useful, useful, useful, useful, useful, visit us at the tradeshow...*

Get Employees to Post Your Content as Well as Your Company Page

And remember, LinkedIn marketing is a **team sport**: if you have a great blog post, video, or infographic, have it posted not only to your company LinkedIn page but have key employees share it as an update on their own LinkedIn profile as well!

In other words, make 80% or more of your posts useful, and only 20% or less, shameless, self-promotional announcements. If you like you can "pin" a company update to the top of your company Page. Simply find the update, and click "Pin to top" located beneath it.

Here are some examples of effective LinkedIn company pages:

- Thermo Fischer Scientific at https://www.linkedin.com/company/thermo-fisher-scientific.
- Intel Corporation at https://www.linkedin.com/company/intel-corporation
- Hewlett-Packard at https://www.linkedin.com/company/hewlett-packard

- Monsanto at https://www.linkedin.com/company/monsanto
- Social Media Examiner https://www.linkedin.com/company/social-media-examiner

To find companies to emulate, either search LinkedIn directly by keywords, or use this Google trick. Go to https://www.google.com/ and enter:

site:linkedin.com/company {keyword}

site:linkedin.com/company {company name}

as for example:

site:linkedin.com/company "organic food" at http://bit.ly/1NxviIZ

You'll find that LinkedIn is fast becoming a better home for more "serious" or even "boring" companies than Facebook; companies whose business value proposition is more *business-to-business* rather than *business-to-consumer*, and whose customers engage when they are in their work / professional / business mode.

In sum, if your business is *business-to-business* such as professional services like Web design, accounting, business attorneys, computer services, SEO, social media marketing, marketing services… any business-to-business, professional service, then a company Page on LinkedIn can be a very effective marketing tool.

» PROMOTING YOUR LINKEDIN PROFILES, POSTS, AND PAGES

Once you and your employees have established their individual profiles, begun to share updates or posts to LinkedIn *Pulse*, set up a company Page, and begun to populate it with posts on a regular basis, you've essentially "set up" the social media party. Now it's time to send out the invitations. In and of itself, nothing on LinkedIn is truly self-promotional.

Remember: social media is a **party**. You must have yummy yummy food and entertainment for people to show up, and stick around. So as you promote your LinkedIn **content**, always keep front and center "what's in it for them" – what will they get by connecting with your employees on LinkedIn or following your company LinkedIn page?

Generally speaking, people on LinkedIn are looking for informative, educational, useful, professional content relevant to their industry and job, so that they can stay informed and educated. If on Facebook the name of the game is *fun*, on LinkedIn the name of the game is *useful*.

FACEBOOK IS ABOUT FUN; LINKEDIN IS ABOUT USEFUL

Assuming your profiles and Page have lots of useful content, here are some common ways to promote your LinkedIn accounts:

- **Real World to Social.** Don't forget the real world! If you are a serious technology vendor of single board computers, and you're at the industry trade show, be sure that the folks manning the booth, recommend to booth visitors that they "connect" with your employees and "follow" your business LinkedIn Page. *Why? Because they'll get insider tips, industry news, free eBooks and webinars – stuff that will keep them abreast of the industry, and better informed at their jobs.*
- **Cross-Promotion**. Link your website to your LinkedIn profiles and Page, your blog posts to your profiles and Page, your Twitter to your profiles and Page, etc. Notice how big brands like Intel (http://www.intel.com/) do this: one digital property promotes another digital property.
- **Email**. Email your customer list and ask them to "connect" with key employees and/or "follow" your Page. Again, you must have a reason why they'll should do so: what's in it for them? Have a contest, give away something for free, or otherwise motivate them to click from the email to your profiles or Page, and then connect.
- **LinkedIn Internal**. More at the profile level than on the Page level, participation on LinkedIn in an authentic way can grow one's follower base. LinkedIn *Pulse* is especially useful for this, as are LinkedIn groups. Internal promotion is not particularly strong on LinkedIn, but it should still be in the mix.
- **Use LinkedIn Plugins**. LinkedIn has numerous plugins that allow you to "embed" your LinkedIn content on your website, and thereby nurture cross promotion. To learn more about plugins, visit https://developer.linkedin.com/plugins. In this way, your blog can promote your

LinkedIn content, and your LinkedIn content can promote your blog. Similarly, your YouTube videos can promote your LinkedIn Page, and your LinkedIn updates and *Pulse* posts can promote your YouTube Videos and vice-versa.

- **Leverage your Customers**. People who already have connected with you and your company are your best promoters. Remember, it's *social* (!) media, and encouraging your customers to share your content is the name of the game. You want to leverage your connections as much as possible to share your content. On LinkedIn, it's all about being useful! Indeed, a timely post to LinkedIn *Pulse* can be picked up by key influencers, go viral, and exponentially increase your personal and company reach.

GET YOUR CUSTOMERS TO HELP PROMOTE YOUR LINKEDIN CONTENT

Advertise. Advertising is increasingly important to success on LinkedIn. Visit LinkedIn's advertising center at https://www.linkedin.com/advertising to view their official information. Here are some ideas:

Promote your Page Updates. On your LinkedIn company page, find an update. At the bottom of the update, click on the gray "Sponsor Update" button and follow the instructions. You can demographically target advertising on LinkedIn in a very focused way: people who are members of a group, people who follow specific companies, etc.

Advertise Directly. You can create direct ads on LinkedIn to promote either offsite web content, or connect back to your Page or Posts. In terms of LinkedIn promotion, therefore, you can use LinkedIn advertising to grow your LinkedIn company followers by advertising your Page and/or posts.

Think Out of the Box on LinkedIn Advertising

LinkedIn does not currently allow you to promote individual profiles or the updates / posts of individuals via direct advertising. However, assuming you want to grow the LinkedIn presence of key company employees:

1. Have the employee **post** to his or her **blog**; and/or
   - Have the employee **post** to **LinkedIn** *Pulse*.
2. **Share** this content as an "**update**" via your LinkedIn Page.
3. **Pay to advertise** this content via your Company Account by clicking the "Sponsor Update" button.

In this way, you can use your company Page to grow the following of individual key employees as well as boost their content for thought-leadership and brand purposes.

» MEASURING YOUR RESULTS

LinkedIn offers more metrics at the company level than at the personal profile level.

LinkedIn Profiles

First, let's look at the profile level. If you have a free account, login to your LinkedIn profile and then click the "Who's viewed your profile" section on the right. That gets you to LinkedIn stats, such as who has viewed your profile, your posts, and a comparison of how your rank for profile views compared with those of similar people on LinkedIn. Here's a screenshot:

If you click on the center tab, "Who's viewed your posts," this gives you metrics for your LinkedIn Pulse posts. Here you find detailed information on their industries, job titles, locations, and traffic sources. If they interacted with your post by liking, commenting on, or sharing it, then you can also click up to their LinkedIn profile to learn more about them. Indeed, this even gives you an excuse to reach out and connect. By paying and joining LinkedIn premium (https://premium.linkedin.com/), you gain access to more detailed data.

As for your shared updates, the only data available is to look at each update and eyeball how many comments and likes an update received. By clicking on the like, comment, or share icon, you can see who interacted with an update.

LinkedIn Pages

LinkedIn Page data is more robust. If you are logged in as the company, simply scroll down to company updates. For each, you can see impressions, clicks, interactions, and engagement data.

Click on the "Analytics" tab and LinkedIn provides lots of graphical data about your Page and its reach. Click on "Notifications," and you can see likes, comments, shares, and mentions in more detail.

Google Analytics

For many of us, we want to drive traffic from LinkedIn to our website, even to our ecommerce store or to download a free eBook or software package to get a sales lead. Sign up for Google Analytics (https://www.google.com/analytics) and install the required tracking code. Inside of your Google Analytics account on the left column, drill down by clicking on Acquisition > Social > Overview. Then on the right hand side of the screen you'll see a list of Social Networks. Find LinkedIn on that list, and click on that. Google Analytics will tell you what URLs people clicked to from LinkedIn to your Website, giving you insights into what types of web content people find attractive.

You can also create a custom Advanced Segment to look at only LinkedIn traffic and its behavior. For information on how to create custom Advanced Segments in Google Analytics, go to http://jmlinks.com/1f. For the Google help files on Advanced Segments go to http://jmlinks.com/1g.

In sum, inside of LinkedIn you can see how people interact with your Page and updates as well as those made by individual profiles. Inside of Google Analytics, you can see where they land on your website and what they do after they arrive.

» DELIVERABLE: A LINKEDIN MARKETING PLAN

Now that we've come to the end our chapter on LinkedIn, your **DELIVERABLE** has arrived. For your final **TODO**, download the **LinkedIn Marketing Plan Worksheet**. For the worksheet, go to https://www.jm-seo.org/workbooks (click on LinkedIn, enter the code 'linkedin2016' to register if you have not already done so), and click on the link to the "LinkedIn Marketing Plan Worksheet." You'll brainstorm your strategy for LinkedIn at both the employee (profile) and company (Page) level.

» TOP TEN LINKEDIN MARKETING TOOLS AND RESOURCES

Here are the top ten tools and resources to help you with LinkedIn marketing. For an up-to-date list, go to https://www.jm-seo.org/workbooks (click on LinkedIn, enter the code 'linkedin2016' to register if you have not already done so), and click on the link to the *Social Media Toolbook* link, and drill down to the LinkedIn chapter.

LINKEDIN HELP CENTER - http://help.linkedin.com

> Learn about all the different features on LinkedIn. From a brief overview to detailed tips, you'll find them here. Learn about profiles. Find out how to get a new job. Use LinkedIn on your mobile phone. Learn how to build your network. Get answers to your questions with Answers.
>
> **Rating:** 5 Stars | **Category:** overview

LINKEDIN COMPANY PAGES FAQ - http://linkd.in/1BbOokZ

Interested in setting up a business page on LinkedIn? Here's the official FAQ on LinkedIn company pages.

Rating: 4 Stars | **Category:** resource

LINKEDIN ENGINEERING - http://engineering.linkedin.com

LinkedIn Engineering hosts a small set of projects and experimental features built by the employees of LinkedIn. Some of these plugins can be good for your LinkedIn marketing efforts.

Rating: 4 Stars | **Category:** tool

LINKEDIN YOUTUBE CHANNEL - http://youtube.com/LinkedIn

LinkedIn has some novel advertising opportunities. This is their official YouTube channel. It's pretty salesy, but has some useful information especially on marketing and sales aspects of LinkedIn.

Rating: 4 Stars | **Category:** video

RAPPORTIVE - http://rapportive.com

Rapportive is a Gmail plugin that works with LinkedIn (and other social media sites). So when you're exchanging email with someone, you can see their LinkedIn profile details. It's sort of a bye-bye privacy app that helps you know how 'important' someone is with whom you are interacting.

Rating: 4 Stars | **Category:** tool

OFFICIAL LINKEDIN BLOG - http://blog.linkedin.com

The official LinkedIn Blog...lots of detailed information on what's happening when, where, and how on LinkedIn by LinkedIn staff.

Rating: 4 Stars | **Category:** blog

LINKEDIN MARKETING & ADVERTISING SOLUTIONS - http://business.linkedin.com/marketing-solutions

LinkedIn advertising, like Facebook advertising and unlike Google AdWords, is demographically based. Identify your target customer based on gender, interests, groups they belong to, etc., then set up your pay-per-click advertising.

Rating: 3 Stars | **Category:** service

LINKEDIN PLUGINS - http://developer.linkedin.com/plugins

Want to cross-promote your LinkedIn page from your website? Here's how. Use this page to find the nifty, official LinkedIn plugins. Share on LinkedIn, or follow us on LinkedIn. If you are in HR, you can even have an 'apply' via LinkedIn button. Cool!

Rating: 3 Stars | **Category:** tool

LINKEDIN ON FACEBOOK - http://facebook.com/LinkedIn

Is LinkedIn on Facebook? Doesn't that sound crazy? Connect with LinkedIn on Facebook for the funner side of business networking at the official LinkedIn page on Facebook.

Rating: 3 Stars | **Category:** resource

FIVE HUNDRED PLUS - http://fivehundredplus.com

Five Hundred Plus is an application that uses LinkedIn to help you make the most of your most valuable connections. You may have heard of Customer Relationship Management (CRM) applications used by companies to manage clients and leads. Five Hundred Plus is inspired by those tools but focuses on your own personal network, not your company's.

Rating: 3 Stars | **Category:** tool

LINKEDIN TOOLS

As the top social network for business-to-business, LinkedIn has a cornucopia of free resources and free tools to make your life easier. Below I produce my favorite tools and resources (in rank order). Remember that by registering your copy of the workbook, you can access the *Social Media Toolbook*, which has all the tools in convenient, clickable PDF format. To register, go to https://www.jm-seo.org/workbooks (click on LinkedIn, enter the code 'linkedin2016' to register if you have not already done so), and click on the link to the *Social Media Toolbook*.

Here are free LinkedIn tools and resources, sorted with the best items first.

LINKEDIN HELP CENTER - http://help.linkedin.com

> Learn about all the different features on LinkedIn. From a brief overview to detailed tips, you'll find them here. Learn about profiles. Find out how to get a new job. Use LinkedIn on your mobile phone. Learn how to build your network. Get answers to your questions with Answers.
>
> **Rating:** 5 Stars | **Category:** overview

LINKEDIN COMPANY PAGES FAQ - http://linkd.in/1BbOokZ

> Interested in setting up a business page on LinkedIn? Here's the official FAQ on LinkedIn company pages.

Rating: 4 Stars | **Category:** resource

LINKEDIN ENGINEERING - http://engineering.linkedin.com

LinkedIn Engineering hosts a small set of projects and experimental features built by the employees of LinkedIn. Some of these plugins can be good for your LinkedIn marketing efforts.

Rating: 4 Stars | **Category:** tool

LINKEDIN YOUTUBE CHANNEL - http://youtube.com/LinkedIn

LinkedIn has some novel advertising opportunities. This is their official YouTube channel. It's pretty salesy, but has some useful information especially on marketing and sales aspects of LinkedIn.

Rating: 4 Stars | **Category:** video

SMALL BUSINESS GUIDE TO LINKEDIN - http://simplybusiness.co.uk/microsites/linkedin-guide

Interactive step-by-step guide to using LinkedIn for small business. Comprised of key questions and linked resources from around the web with more information. Follow this step-by-step guide and make LinkedIn an effective part of your marketing strategy.

Rating: 4 Stars | **Category:** resource

RAPPORTIVE - http://rapportive.com

Rapportive is a Gmail plugin that works with LinkedIn (and other social media sites). So when you're exchanging email with someone, you can see their LinkedIn profile details. It's sort of a bye-bye privacy app that helps you know how 'important' someone is with whom you are interacting.

Rating: 4 Stars | **Category:** tool

LINKEDIN COMPANY DIRECTORY - http://linkedin.com/directory/companies

Looking for ideas for your LinkedIn company page? Here is a handy directory of the cool companies on LinkedIn by industry.

Rating: 4 Stars | **Category:** resource

LINKEDIN PULSE - https://www.linkedin.com/today/posts

Need ideas for your next blog post? Look no further than LinkedIn Pulse where top business influencers post their thoughts daily. Handy drop-down selector at right allows you to see Top Posts from today, this week, and all time. Click the Discover Tab to customize your Pulse feed with influencers relevant to your interests.

Rating: 4 Stars | **Category:** resource

OFFICIAL LINKEDIN BLOG - http://blog.linkedin.com

The official LinkedIn Blog...lots of detailed information on what's happening when, where, and how on LinkedIn by LinkedIn staff.

Rating: 4 Stars | **Category:** blog

LINKEDIN MARKETING & ADVERTISING SOLUTIONS - http://business.linkedin.com/marketing-solutions

LinkedIn advertising, like Facebook advertising and unlike Google AdWords, is demographically based. Identify your target customer based on gender, interests, groups they belong to, etc., then set up your pay-per-click advertising.

Rating: 3 Stars | **Category:** service

LINKEDIN PLUGINS - http://developer.linkedin.com/plugins

Want to cross-promote your LinkedIn page from your website? Here's how. Use this page to find the nifty, official LinkedIn plugins. Share on LinkedIn, or follow us on LinkedIn. If you are in HR, you can even have an 'apply' via LinkedIn button. Cool!

Rating: 3 Stars | **Category:** tool

LINKEDIN ON FACEBOOK - http://facebook.com/LinkedIn

Is LinkedIn on Facebook? Doesn't that sound crazy? Connect with LinkedIn on Facebook for the funner side of business networking at the official LinkedIn page on Facebook.

Rating: 3 Stars | **Category:** resource

FIVE HUNDRED PLUS - http://fivehundredplus.com

Five Hundred Plus is an application that uses LinkedIn to help you make the most of your most valuable connections. You may have heard of Customer Relationship Management (CRM) applications used by companies to manage clients and leads. Five Hundred Plus is inspired by those tools but focuses on your own personal network, not your company's.

Rating: 3 Stars | **Category:** tool

HOW TO USE TWITTER ON LINKEDIN -
http://help.linkedin.com/app/answers/detail/a_id/2754

What goes better than chocolate and peanut butter? LinkedIn and Twitter, of course. Start here to learn how to integrate Twitter on LinkedIn.

Rating: 3 Stars | **Category:** resource

LINKEDIN SHOWCASE PAGES - http://linkd.in/11NWFJd

Finally! LinkedIn has added some clever functionality to brand pages on LinkedIn. You can add a 'Showcase' page that might be a specific product line, theme, or topic. Then this 'page' can share information with followers just like a complete page. Great if your business has individual product lines or topics.

Rating: 3 Stars | **Category:** tool

LINKEDIN HELP YOUTUBE CHANNEL - http://youtube.com/linkedinhelp

The helpful folks at LinkedIn customer support have their own YouTube channel. Watch, learn, and participate in video learning on how to be a better LinkedIn user.

Rating: 3 Stars | **Category:** resource

LINKEDIN ON TWITTER - https://twitter.com/LinkedIn

Yes, LinkedIn is on Twitter. So follow LinkedIn on Twitter for instant updates on LinkedIn about LinkedIn.

Rating: 3 Stars | **Category:** resource

LINKEDIN MOBILE - https://www.linkedin.com/mobile

LinkedIn has just a few tools, but if you are a power LinkedIn user, these tools can help you search LinkedIn from your Google toolbar, import your contacts and perform other functions to help leverage your network for LinkedIn marketing. Primarily for your phone.

Rating: 3 Stars | **Category:** tool

LINKEDIN LEARNING WEBINARS - http://help.linkedin.com/app/answers/detail/a_id/530

LinkedIn hosts live learning webinars on a variety of timely LinkedIn topics. Alternatively, users can view pre-recorded sessions. Topics are designed for a variety of audiences including, job seekers, corporate communications professionals, and journalists.

Rating: 3 Stars | **Category:** resource

LINKEDIN COMPANY PAGE ANALYTICS - http://simplymeasured.com/freebies/linkedin-profile-analytics

This free report from social media analytics company Simply Measured answers questions about your LinkedIn Company Page performance and engagement, analyzes attributes of key influencers interacting with your content, and measures the effectiveness of content by post date.

Rating: 2 Stars | **Category:** tool

Made in the USA
Columbia, SC
11 August 2021